BIRDS
A SECRET LIFE

A disguised password book and personal
internet address log for bird lovers

Ceri Clark

BIRDS A Secret life: A disguised password book and personal internet address log for bird lovers

© 2016 Cover & Interior Design: Ceri Clark

First Edition
ISBN-10: 1-68063-039-3
ISBN-13: 978-1-68063-039-8
Published by
Myrddin Publishing Group
Contact us at - www.myrddinpublishing.com

Myrddin Publishing

unique electronic & print books

Images from royalty free collection and
© Can Stock Photo Inc. / Nejron

Are you always forgetting or losing your passwords? Are you worried about having a password organizer that screams "steal me" if you get burgled? Would you like a password book but you want something a little different?

If this sounds familiar, then this book was made for you. The cover is designed so it won't get noticed by thieves who are looking for an obvious password logbook. Of course it is also protected from online thieves by being a paperback! Simply slip this volume into your bookshelves with other books to hide it in plain sight.

There is a risk that if someone steals this or any other password keeper then they can get into your internet accounts. For this reason, please keep this book safe and secure and hidden at home.

To help you, this section shares tips for creating a secure password. This will make it difficult for anyone to get into your accounts even if they get this book.

How to Choose a Password

First of all, your password needs to be strong. Whatever you choose, there should be at least 8 characters in your password. If possible, these should be a mixture of lower and uppercase letters, numbers and special characters such as a $, *, &, @ etc.

The secret to using this book with this tip is that you only write down half of the password in this book. What you record needs to be random with a combination of characters. The reason that this method is secure is that half of the password is (only) stored in your head. It does not matter where you put the memorized half of the password into the complete password. This can be at the beginning, middle or end, as long as it is not written down and is consistent so you remember it. The box shows how this can work in practice.

As you can see this would be difficult to guess. You should not store it in an online password vault service unless you put it behind something protected by 2-step authentication.

> **Example**
> Memorized half (only in your head):
> wind
> Recorded half (in spreadsheet):
> Hydf54j@#f
> Full password while logging in:
> windHydf54j@#f

Other ways to write down your password could be to use a code or have a theme but these can be very difficult to remember or will involve so much time to work it out that you will end up writing the real password anyway. The advantage of the above method is that you only need to remember the one 'password', albeit half a password but every password will still be different.

Bonus Tip

2-step verification/ authentication is an extra step to make sure that access to your information, files and folders on an online service is restricted to you. Instead of relying on a password (which might be gained through nefarious means by hackers from a website or other ways), a second device is used which you always have on you such as a phone, tablet computer or key ring. Using the 2-step verification method along with a secure password would mean any would-be infiltrator, bent on your destruction would need to have your password from this book, the memorized word from your mind AND your phone to gain access to your account.

For an example of how to setup 2-step verification, please download my free e-book, A Simpler Guide to Online Security, available at all good online retailers (paperback also available) from:

http://cericlark.com/Ae

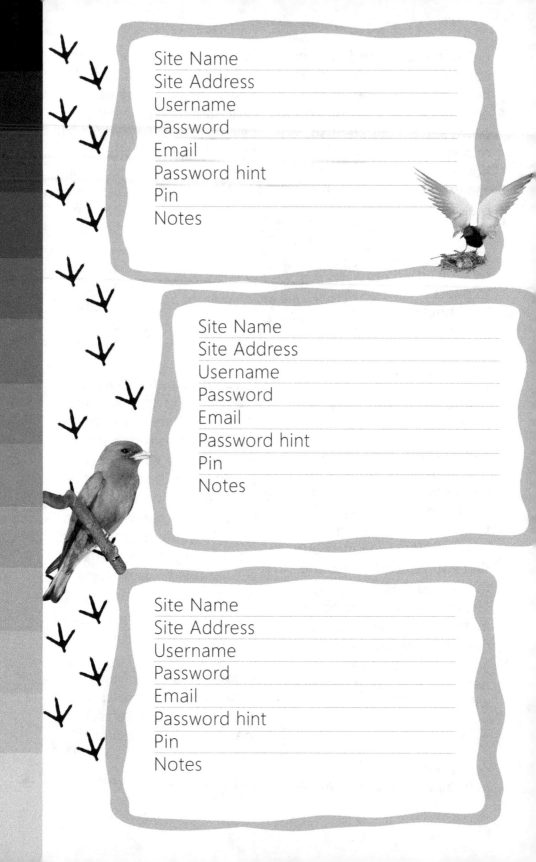

Site Name
Site Address
Username
Password
Email
Password hint
Pin
Notes

Site Name
Site Address
Username
Password
Email
Password hint
Pin
Notes

Site Name
Site Address
Username
Password
Email
Password hint
Pin
Notes

Site Name

Site Address

Username

Password

Email

Password hint

Pin

Notes

Site Name

Site Address

Username

Password

Email

Password hint ..

Pin

Notes

Site Name

Site Address

Username

Password

Email

Password hint

Pin

Notes

A-B

C-D

E-F

G-H

I-J

K-L

M-N

O-P

Q-R

S-T

U-V

W-X

Y-Z

Site Name
Site Address
Username
Password
Email
Password hint
Pin
Notes

Site Name
Site Address
Username
Password
Email
Password hint
Pin
Notes

Site Name
Site Address
Username
Password
Email
Password hint
Pin
Notes

Site Name

Site Address

Username

Password

Email

Password hint

Pin

Notes

Site Name

Site Address

Username

Password

Email

Password hint ..

Pin

Notes

Site Name

Site Address

Username

Password

Email

Password hint

Pin

Notes

A-B

C-D

E-F

G-H

I-J

K-L

M-N

O-P

Q-R

S-T

U-V

W-X

Y-Z

Site Name
Site Address
Username
Password
Email
Password hint
Pin
Notes

Site Name
Site Address
Username
Password
Email
Password hint
Pin
Notes

Site Name
Site Address
Username
Password
Email
Password hint
Pin
Notes

Site Name
Site Address
Username
Password
Email
Password hint
Pin
Notes

Site Name
Site Address
Username
Password
Email
Password hint ..
Pin
Notes

Site Name
Site Address
Username
Password
Email
Password hint
Pin
Notes

A-B

C-D

E-F

G-H

I-J

K-L

M-N

O-P

Q-R

S-T

U-V

W-X

Y-Z

Site Name

Site Address

Username

Password

Email

Password hint

Pin

Notes

Site Name

Site Address

Username

Password

Email

Password hint

Pin

Notes

Site Name

Site Address

Username

Password

Email

Password hint

Pin

Notes

Site Name
Site Address
Username
Password
Email
Password hint
Pin
Notes

Site Name
Site Address
Username
Password
Email
Password hint ..
Pin
Notes

Site Name
Site Address
Username
Password
Email
Password hint
Pin
Notes

A-B

C-D

E-F

G-H

I-J

K-L

M-N

O-P

Q-R

S-T

U-V

W-X

Y-Z

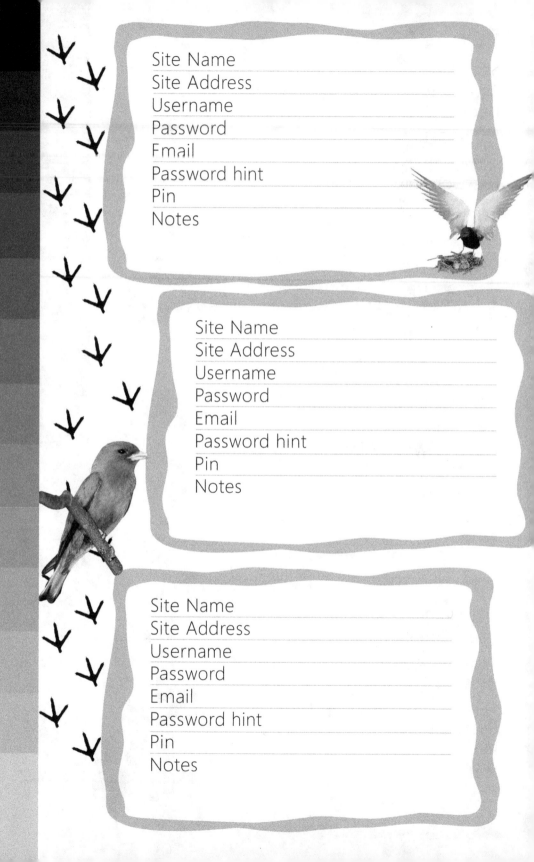

Site Name

Site Address

Username

Password

Fmail

Password hint

Pin

Notes

Site Name

Site Address

Username

Password

Email

Password hint

Pin

Notes

Site Name

Site Address

Username

Password

Email

Password hint

Pin

Notes

Site Name
Site Address
Username
Password
Email
Password hint
Pin
Notes

Site Name
Site Address
Username
Password
Email
Password hint ..
Pin
Notes

Site Name
Site Address
Username
Password
Email
Password hint
Pin
Notes

A-B

C-D

E-F

G-H

I-J

K-L

M-N

O-P

Q-R

S-T

U-V

W-X

Y-Z

Site Name Credit Camera
Site Address
Username
Password Maga Joan 74
Email
Password hint 5946
Pin
Notes

Site Name
Site Address
Username
Password
Email
Password hint
Pin
Notes

Site Name
Site Address
Username
Password
Email
Password hint
Pin
Notes

Site Name

Site Address

Username

Password

Email

Password hint

Pin

Notes

Site Name

Site Address

Username

Password

Email

Password hint

Pin

Notes

Site Name

Site Address

Username

Password

Email

Password hint

Pin

Notes

C-D

E-F

G-H

I-J

K-L

M-N

O-P

Q-R

S-T

U-V

W-X

Y-Z

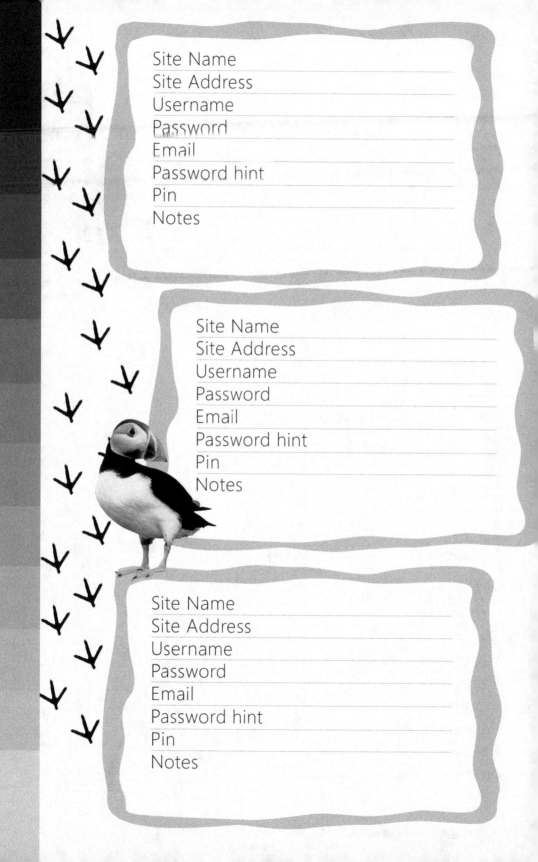

Site Name
Site Address
Username
Password
Email
Password hint
Pin
Notes

Site Name
Site Address
Username
Password
Email
Password hint
Pin
Notes

Site Name
Site Address
Username
Password
Email
Password hint
Pin
Notes

Site Name
Site Address
Username
Password
Email
Password hint
Pin
Notes

Site Name
Site Address
Username
Password
Email
Password hint
Pin
Notes

Site Name
Site Address
Username
Password
Email
Password hint
Pin
Notes

C-D

E-F

G-H

I-J

K-L

M-N

O-P

Q-R

S-T

U-V

W-X

Y-Z

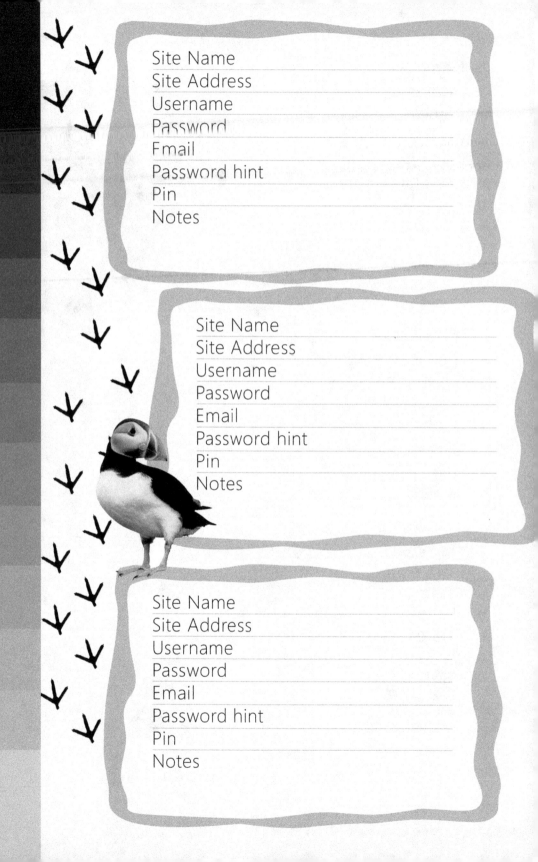

Site Name
Site Address
Username
Password
Fmail
Password hint
Pin
Notes

Site Name
Site Address
Username
Password
Email
Password hint
Pin
Notes

Site Name
Site Address
Username
Password
Email
Password hint
Pin
Notes

Site Name
Site Address
Username
Password
Email
Password hint
Pin
Notes

Site Name
Site Address
Username
Password
Email
Password hint
Pin
Notes

Site Name
Site Address
Username
Password
Email
Password hint
Pin
Notes

C-D

E-F

G-H

I-J

K-L

M-N

O-P

Q-R

S-T

U-V

W-X

Y-Z

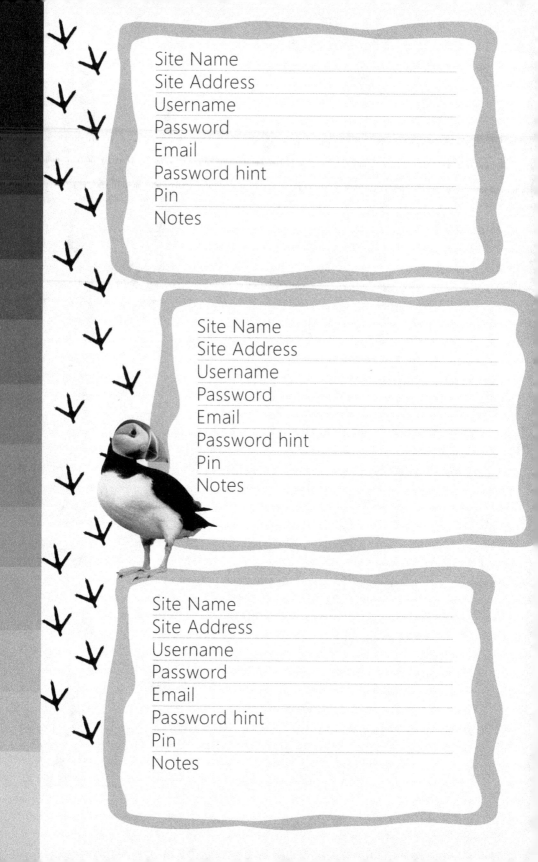

Site Name

Site Address

Username

Password

Email

Password hint

Pin

Notes

Site Name

Site Address

Username

Password

Email

Password hint

Pin

Notes

Site Name

Site Address

Username

Password

Email

Password hint

Pin

Notes

Site Name
Site Address
Username
Password
Email
Password hint
Pin
Notes

Site Name
Site Address
Username
Password
Email
Password hint
Pin
Notes

Site Name
Site Address
Username
Password
Email
Password hint
Pin
Notes

C-D

E-F

G-H

I-J

K-L

M-N

O-P

Q-R

S-T

U-V

W-X

Y-Z

Site Name

Site Address

Username

Password

Email

Password hint

Pin

Notes

Site Name

Site Address

Username

Password

Email

Password hint

Pin

Notes

Site Name

Site Address

Username

Password

Email

Password hint

Pin

Notes

Site Name

Site Address

Username

Password

Email

Password hint

Pin

Notes

Site Name

Site Address

Username

Password

Email

Password hint

Pin

Notes

Site Name

Site Address

Username

Password

Email

Password hint

Pin

Notes

C-D

E-F

G-H

I-J

K-L

M-N

O-P

Q-R

S-T

U-V

W-X

Y-Z

Site Name

Site Address

Username

Password

Email

Password hint

Pin

Notes

Site Name

Site Address

Username

Password

Email

Password hint

Pin

Notes

Site Name

Site Address

Username

Password

Email

Password hint

Pin

Notes

Site Name
Site Address
Username
Password
Email
Password hint
Pin
Notes

Site Name
Site Address
Username
Password
Email
Password hint
Pin
Notes

Site Name
Site Address
Username
Password
Email
Password hint
Pin
Notes

E-F

G-H

I-J

K-L

M-N

O-P

Q-R

S-T

U-V

W-X

Y-Z

Site Name

Site Address

Username

Password

Email

Password hint

Pin

Notes

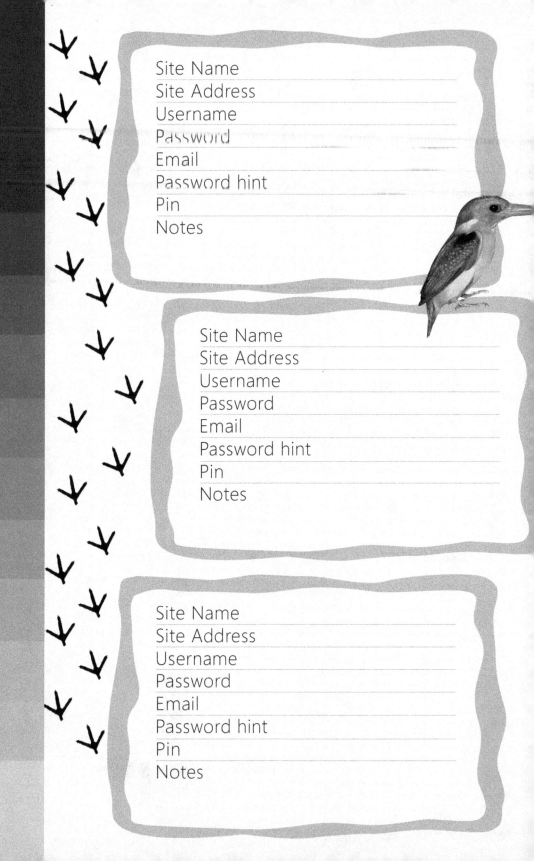

Site Name

Site Address

Username

Password

Email

Password hint

Pin

Notes

Site Name

Site Address

Username

Password

Email

Password hint

Pin

Notes

Site Name

Site Address

Username

Password

Email

Password hint

Pin

Notes

Site Name

Site Address

Username

Password

Email

Password hint

Pin

Notes

Site Name

Site Address

Username

Password

Email

Password hint

Pin

Notes

E-F

G-H

I-J

K-L

M-N

O-P

Q-R

S-T

U-V

W-X

Y-Z

Site Name

Site Address

Username

Password

Email

Password hint

Pin

Notes

Site Name

Site Address

Username

Password

Email

Password hint

Pin

Notes

Site Name

Site Address

Username

Password

Email

Password hint

Pin

Notes

Site Name

Site Address

Username

Password

Email

Password hint

Pin

Notes

Site Name

Site Address

Username

Password

Email

Password hint

Pin

Notes

Site Name

Site Address

Username

Password

Email

Password hint

Pin

Notes

E-F

G-H

I-J

K-L

M-N

O-P

Q-R

S-T

U-V

W-X

Y-Z

Site Name
Site Address
Username
Password
Email
Password hint
Pin
Notes

Site Name
Site Address
Username
Password
Email
Password hint
Pin
Notes

Site Name
Site Address
Username
Password
Email
Password hint
Pin
Notes

Site Name

Site Address

Username

Password

Email

Password hint

Pin

Notes

Site Name

Site Address

Username

Password

Email

Password hint

Pin

Notes

Site Name

Site Address

Username

Password

Email

Password hint

Pin

Notes

E-F

G-H

I-J

K-L

M-N

O-P

Q-R

S-T

U-V

W-X

Y-Z

Site Name
Site Address
Username
Password
Email
Password hint
Pin
Notes

Site Name
Site Address
Username
Password
Email
Password hint
Pin
Notes

Site Name
Site Address
Username
Password
Email
Password hint
Pin
Notes

Site Name

Site Address

Username

Password

Email

Password hint

Pin

Notes

Site Name

Site Address

Username

Password

Email

Password hint

Pin

Notes

Site Name

Site Address

Username

Password

Email

Password hint

Pin

Notes

E-F

G-H

I-J

K-L

M-N

O-P

Q-R

S-T

U-V

W-X

Y-Z

Site Name GICGO INS.
Site Address
Username Joan Paterson
Password DoNate1/486
Email JPanger Werseip@yahoo.com
Password hint sneakers
Pin
Notes Nancy Reiner MANET

Site Name
Site Address
Username
Password
Email
Password hint
Pin
Notes

Site Name Goggles 4U
Site Address
Username   me
Password Record 68=
Email
Password hint 1 888 830 7867
Pin   Eye Glasses
Notes

Site Name
Site Address
Username
Password
Email
Password hint
Pin
Notes

Site Name
Site Address
Username
Password
Email
Password hint
Pin
Notes

Site Name
Site Address
Username
Password
Email
Password hint
Pin
Notes

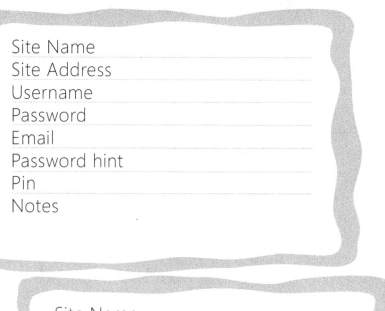

G-H

I-J

K-L

M-N

O-P

Q-R

S-T

U-V

W-X

Y-Z

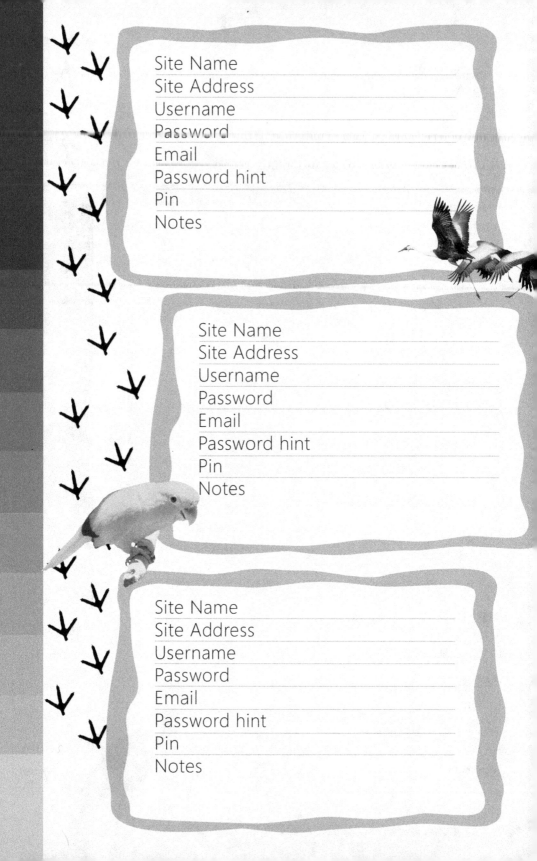

Site Name
Site Address
Username
Password
Email
Password hint
Pin
Notes

Site Name
Site Address
Username
Password
Email
Password hint
Pin
Notes

Site Name
Site Address
Username
Password
Email
Password hint
Pin
Notes

Site Name
Site Address
Username
Password
Email
Password hint
Pin
Notes

Site Name
Site Address
Username
Password
Email
Password hint
Pin
Notes

Site Name
Site Address
Username
Password
Email
Password hint
Pin
Notes

G-H

I-J

K-L

M-N

O-P

Q-R

S-T

U-V

W-X

Y-Z

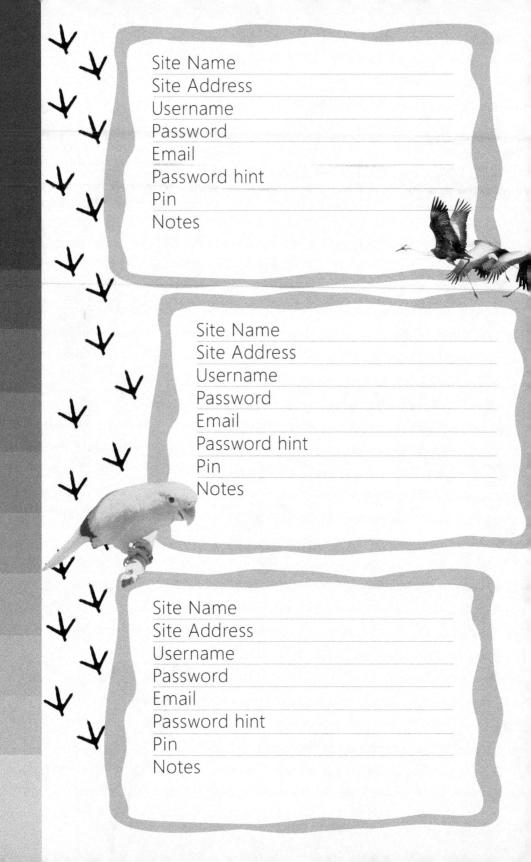

Site Name
Site Address
Username
Password
Email
Password hint
Pin
Notes

Site Name
Site Address
Username
Password
Email
Password hint
Pin
Notes

Site Name
Site Address
Username
Password
Email
Password hint
Pin
Notes

Site Name
Site Address
Username
Password
Email
Password hint
Pin
Notes

Site Name
Site Address
Username
Password
Email
Password hint
Pin
Notes

Site Name
Site Address
Username
Password
Email
Password hint
Pin
Notes

G-H

I-J

K-L

M-N

O-P

Q-R

S-T

U-V

W-X

Y-Z

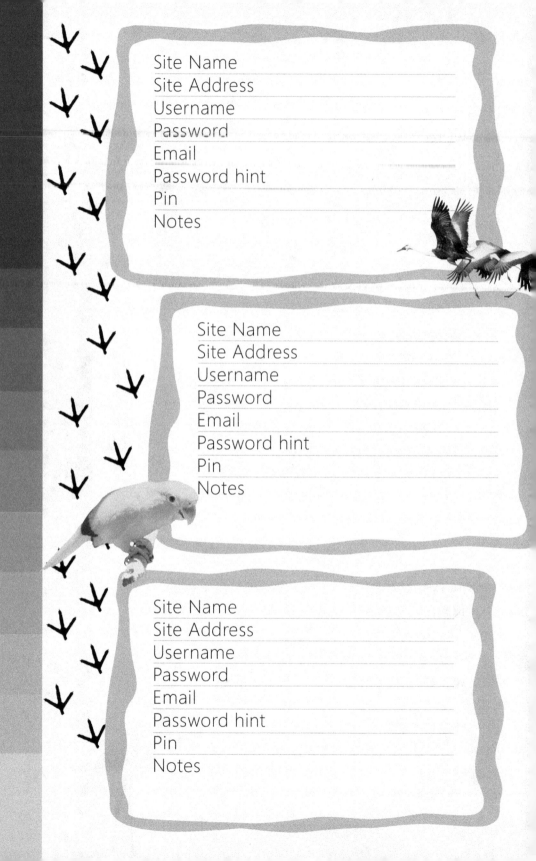

Site Name

Site Address

Username

Password

Email

Password hint

Pin

Notes

Site Name

Site Address

Username

Password

Email

Password hint

Pin

Notes

Site Name

Site Address

Username

Password

Email

Password hint

Pin

Notes

Site Name
Site Address
Username
Password
Email
Password hint
Pin
Notes

Site Name
Site Address
Username
Password
Email
Password hint
Pin
Notes

Site Name
Site Address
Username
Password
Email
Password hint
Pin
Notes

G-H

I-J

K-L

M-N

O-P

Q-R

S-T

U-V

W-X

Y-Z

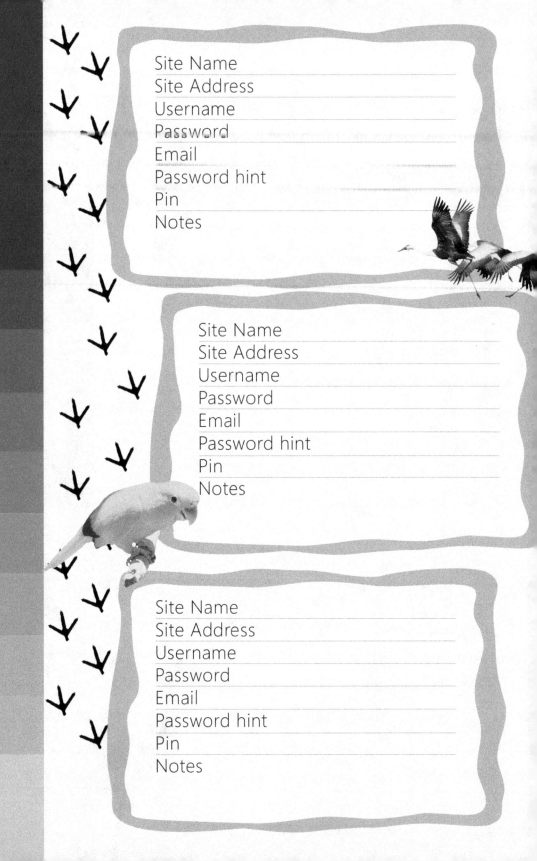

Site Name

Site Address

Username

Password

Email

Password hint

Pin

Notes

Site Name

Site Address

Username

Password

Email

Password hint

Pin

Notes

Site Name

Site Address

Username

Password

Email

Password hint

Pin

Notes

Site Name
Site Address
Username
Password
Email
Password hint
Pin
Notes

Site Name
Site Address
Username
Password
Email
Password hint
Pin
Notes

Site Name
Site Address
Username
Password
Email
Password hint
Pin
Notes

G-H

I-J

K-L

M-N

O-P

Q-R

S-T

U-V

W-X

Y-Z

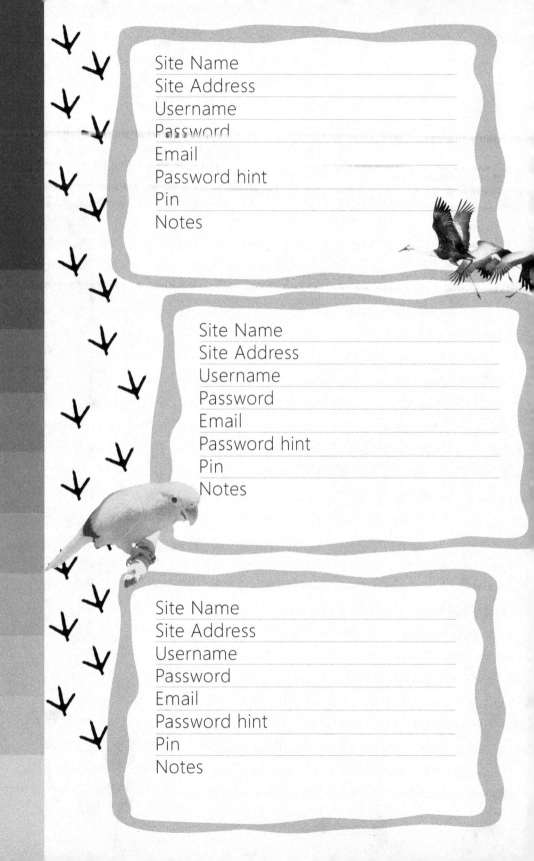

Site Name
Site Address
Username
Password
Email
Password hint
Pin
Notes

Site Name
Site Address
Username
Password
Email
Password hint
Pin
Notes

Site Name
Site Address
Username
Password
Email
Password hint
Pin
Notes

Site Name

Site Address

Username

Password

Email

Password hint

Pin

Notes

Site Name

Site Address

Username

Password

Email

Password hint

Pin

Notes

Site Name

Site Address

Username

Password

Email

Password hint

Pin

Notes

I-J

K-L

M-N

O-P

Q-R

S-T

U-V

W-X

Y-Z

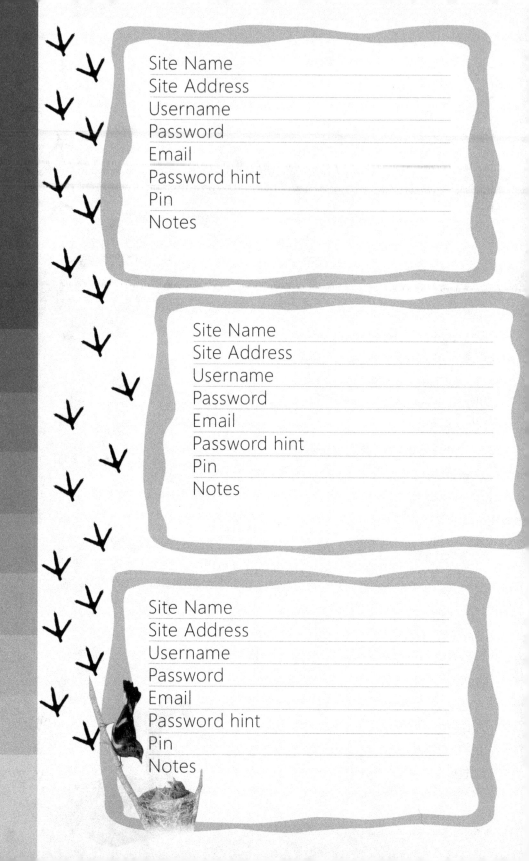

Site Name

Site Address

Username

Password

Email

Password hint

Pin

Notes

Site Name

Site Address

Username

Password

Email

Password hint

Pin

Notes

Site Name

Site Address

Username

Password

Email

Password hint

Pin

Notes

Site Name
Site Address
Username
Password
Email
Password hint
Pin
Notes

Site Name   .
Site Address
Username
Password
Email
Password hint
Pin
Notes

Site Name
Site Address
Username
Password
Email
Password hint
Pin
Notes

I-J

K-L

M-N

O-P

Q-R

S-T

U-V

W-X

Y-Z

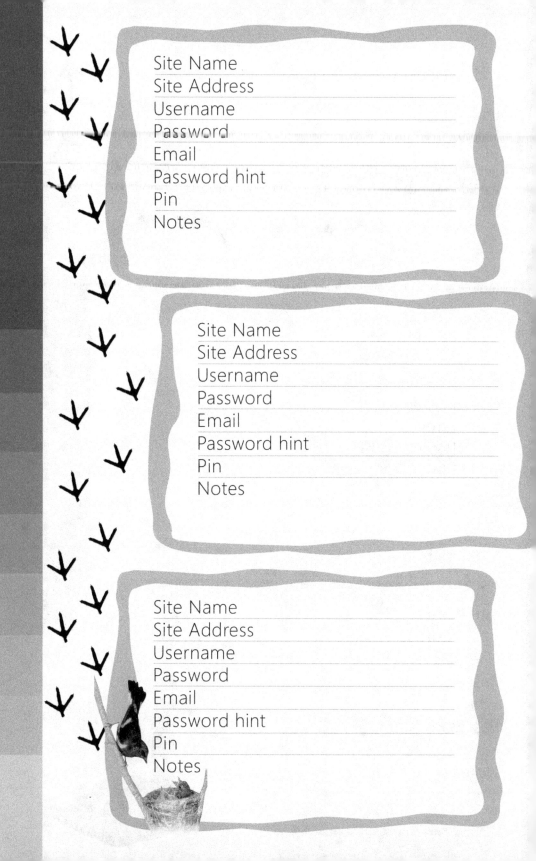

Site Name

Site Address

Username

Password

Email

Password hint

Pin

Notes

Site Name

Site Address

Username

Password

Email

Password hint

Pin

Notes

Site Name

Site Address

Username

Password

Email

Password hint

Pin

Notes

Site Name

Site Address

Username

Password

Email

Password hint

Pin

Notes

Site Name   .

Site Address

Username

Password

Email

Password hint

Pin

Notes

Site Name

Site Address

Username

Password

Email

Password hint

Pin

Notes

I-J

K-L

M-N

O-P

Q-R

S-T

U-V

W-X

Y-Z

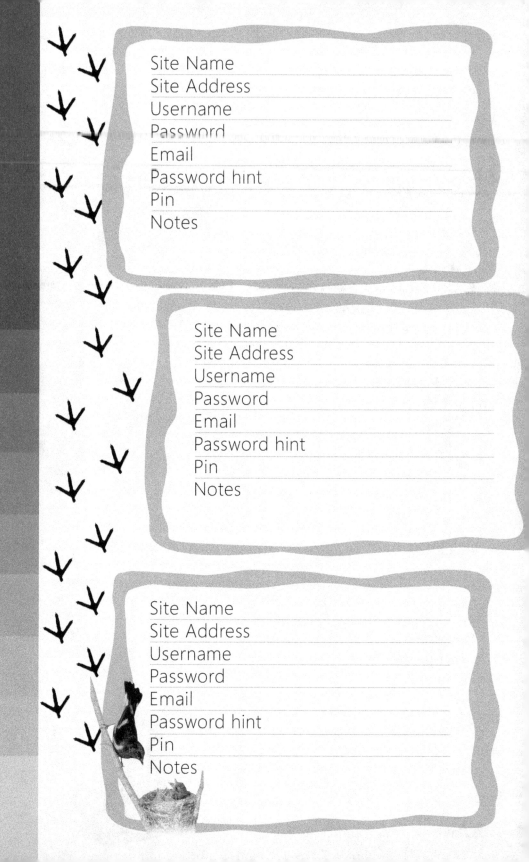

Site Name
Site Address
Username
Password
Email
Password hint
Pin
Notes

Site Name
Site Address
Username
Password
Email
Password hint
Pin
Notes

Site Name
Site Address
Username
Password
Email
Password hint
Pin
Notes

Site Name
Site Address
Username
Password
Email
Password hint
Pin
Notes

Site Name .
Site Address
Username
Password
Email
Password hint
Pin
Notes

Site Name
Site Address
Username
Password
Email
Password hint
Pin
Notes

I-J

K-L

M-N

O-P

Q-R

S-T

U-V

W-X

Y-Z

Site Name
Site Address
Username
Password
Email
Password hint
Pin
Notes

Site Name
Site Address
Username
Password
Email
Password hint
Pin
Notes

Site Name
Site Address
Username
Password
Email
Password hint
Pin
Notes

Site Name
Site Address
Username
Password
Email
Password hint
Pin
Notes

Site Name   .
Site Address
Username
Password
Email
Password hint
Pin
Notes

Site Name
Site Address
Username
Password
Email
Password hint
Pin
Notes

I-J

K-L

M-N

O-P

Q-R

S-T

U-V

W-X

Y-Z

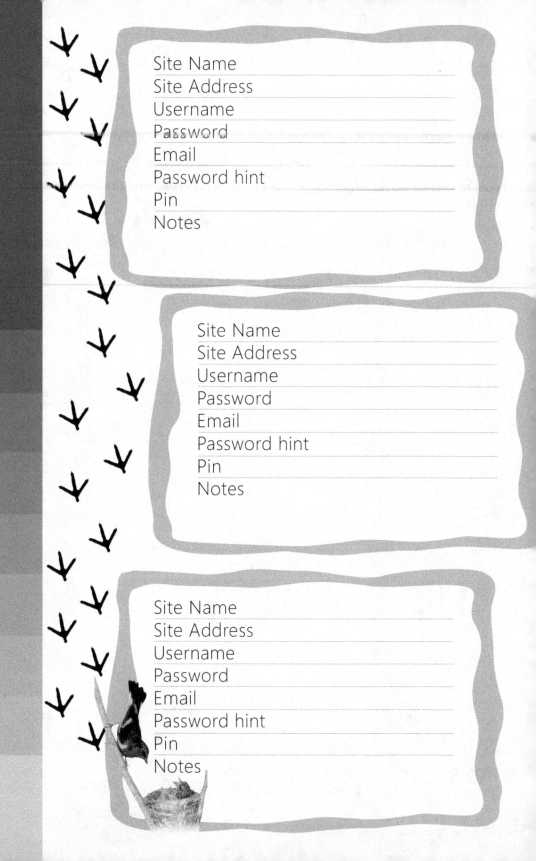

Site Name

Site Address

Username

Password

Email

Password hint

Pin

Notes

Site Name

Site Address

Username

Password

Email

Password hint

Pin

Notes

Site Name

Site Address

Username

Password

Email

Password hint

Pin

Notes

Site Name
Site Address
Username
Password
Email
Password hint
Pin
Notes

Site Name
Site Address
Username
Password
Email
Password hint
Pin
Notes

Site Name
Site Address
Username
Password
Email
Password hint
Pin
Notes

K-L

M-N

O-P

Q-R

S-T

U-V

W-X

Y-Z

Site Name
Site Address
Username
Password
Email
Password hint
Pin
Notes

Site Name
Site Address
Username
Password
Email
Password hint
Pin
Notes

Site Name
Site Address
Username
Password
Email
Password hint
Pin
Notes

Site Name
Site Address
Username
Password
Email
Password hint
Pin
Notes

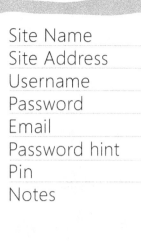

Site Name
Site Address
Username
Password
Email
Password hint
Pin
Notes

Site Name
Site Address
Username
Password
Email
Password hint
Pin
Notes

K-L

M-N

O-P

Q-R

S-T

U-V

W-X

Y-Z

Site Name
Site Address
Username
Password
Email
Password hint
Pin
Notes

Site Name
Site Address
Username
Password
Email
Password hint
Pin
Notes

Site Name
Site Address
Username
Password
Email
Password hint
Pin
Notes

Site Name
Site Address
Username
Password
Email
Password hint
Pin
Notes

Site Name
Site Address
Username
Password
Email
Password hint
Pin
Notes

Site Name
Site Address
Username
Password
Email
Password hint
Pin
Notes

K-L

M-N

O-P

Q-R

S-T

U-V

W-X

Y-Z

Site Name
Site Address
Username
Password
Email
Password hint
Pin
Notes

Site Name
Site Address
Username
Password
Email
Password hint
Pin
Notes

Site Name
Site Address
Username
Password
Email
Password hint
Pin
Notes

Site Name
Site Address
Username
Password
Email
Password hint
Pin
Notes

Site Name
Site Address
Username
Password
Email
Password hint
Pin
Notes

Site Name
Site Address
Username
Password
Email
Password hint
Pin
Notes

K-L

M-N

O-P

Q-R

S-T

U-V

W-X

Y-Z

Site Name

Site Address

Username

Password

Email

Password hint

Pin

Notes

Site Name

Site Address

Username

Password

Email

Password hint

Pin

Notes

Site Name

Site Address

Username

Password

Email

Password hint

Pin

Notes

Site Name
Site Address
Username
Password
Email
Password hint
Pin
Notes

Site Name
Site Address
Username
Password
Email
Password hint
Pin
Notes

Site Name
Site Address
Username
Password
Email
Password hint
Pin
Notes

K-L

M-N

O-P

Q-R

S-T

U-V

W-X

Y-Z

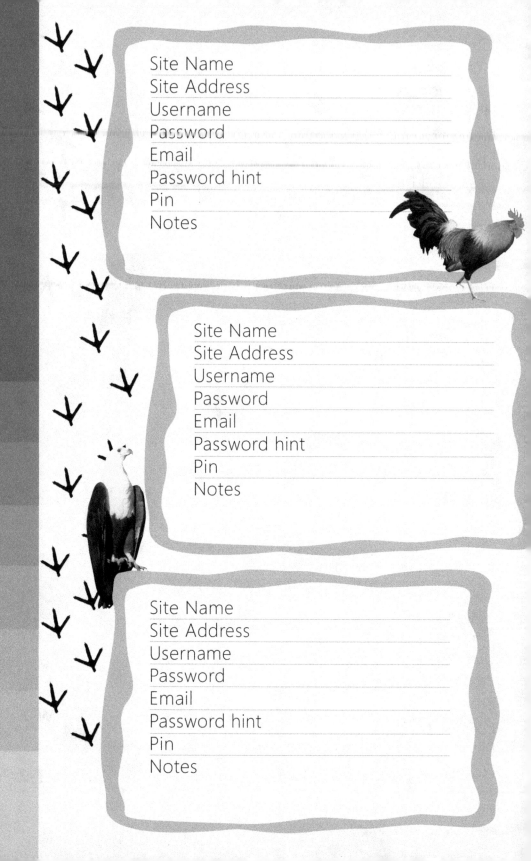

Site Name

Site Address

Username

Password

Email

Password hint

Pin

Notes

Site Name

Site Address

Username

Password

Email

Password hint

Pin

Notes

Site Name

Site Address

Username

Password

Email

Password hint

Pin

Notes

Site Name
Site Address
Username
Password
Email
Password hint
Pin
Notes

Site Name
Site Address
Username
Password
Email
Password hint
Pin
Notes

Site Name
Site Address
Username
Password
Email
Password hint
Pin
Notes

M-N

O-P

Q-R

S-T

U-V

W-X

Y-Z

Site Name

Site Address

Username

Password

Email

Password hint

Pin

Notes

Site Name

Site Address

Username

Password

Email

Password hint

Pin

Notes

Site Name

Site Address

Username

Password

Email

Password hint

Pin

Notes

Site Name
Site Address
Username
Password
Email
Password hint
Pin
Notes

Site Name
Site Address
Username
Password
Email
Password hint
Pin
Notes

Site Name
Site Address
Username
Password
Email
Password hint
Pin
Notes

M-N

O-P

Q-R

S-T

U-V

W-X

Y-Z

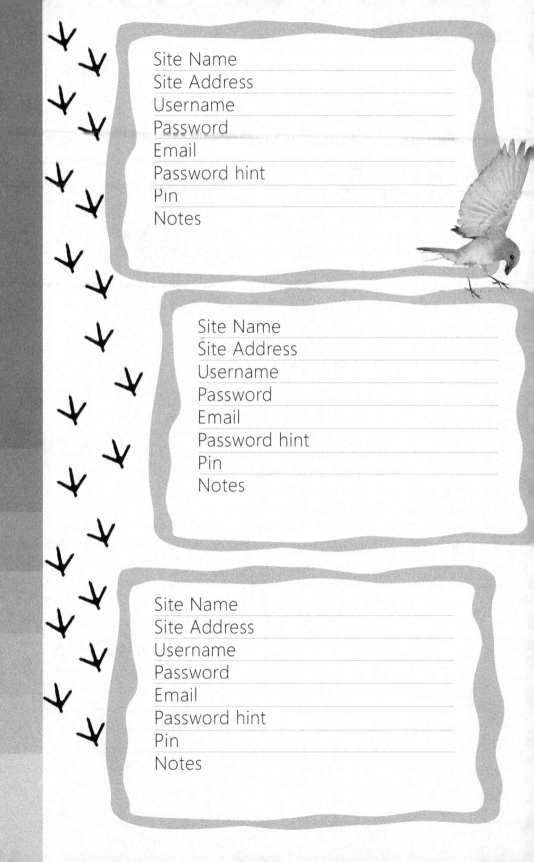

Site Name
Site Address
Username
Password
Email
Password hint
Pin
Notes

Site Name
Site Address
Username
Password
Email
Password hint
Pin
Notes

Site Name
Site Address
Username
Password
Email
Password hint
Pin
Notes

Site Name
Site Address
Username
Password
Email
Password hint
Pin
Notes

Site Name
Site Address
Username
Password
Email
Password hint
Pin
Notes

Site Name
Site Address
Username
Password
Email
Password hint
Pin
Notes

M-N

O-P

Q-R

S-T

U-V

W-X

Y-Z

Site Name

Site Address

Username

Password

Email

Password hint

Pin

Notes

Site Name

Site Address

Username

Password

Email

Password hint

Pin

Notes

Site Name

Site Address

Username

Password

Email

Password hint

Pin

Notes

Site Name
Site Address
Username
Password
Email
Password hint
Pin
Notes

Site Name
Site Address
Username
Password
Email
Password hint
Pin
Notes

Site Name
Site Address
Username
Password
Email
Password hint
Pin
Notes

M-N

O-P

Q-R

S-T

U-V

W-X

Y-Z

Site Name

Site Address

Username

Password

Email

Password hint

Pin

Notes

Site Name

Site Address

Username

Password

Email

Password hint

Pin

Notes

Site Name

Site Address

Username

Password

Email

Password hint

Pin

Notes

Site Name
Site Address
Username
Password
Email
Password hint
Pin
Notes

Site Name
Site Address
Username
Password
Email
Password hint
Pin
Notes

M-N

O-P

Q-R

S-T

U-V

W-X

Y-Z

Site Name
Site Address
Username
Password
Email
Password hint
Pin
Notes

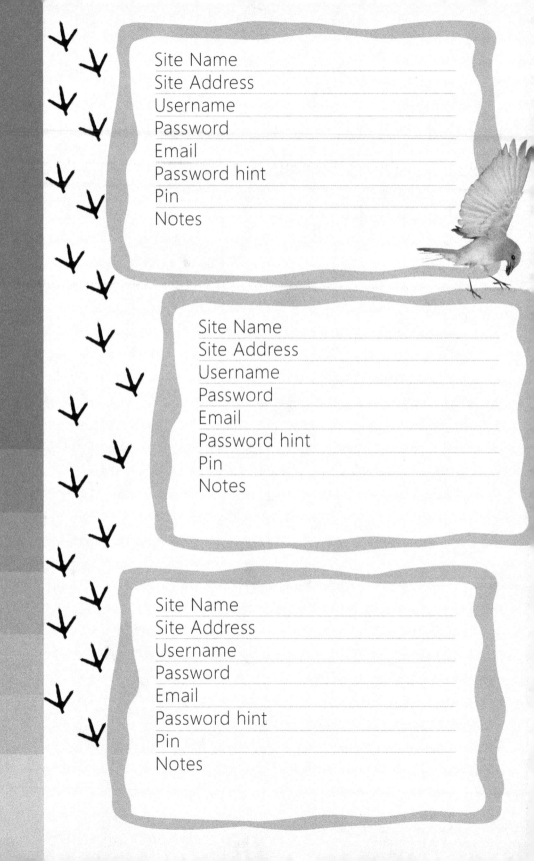

Site Name

Site Address

Username

Password

Email

Password hint

Pin

Notes

Site Name

Site Address

Username

Password

Email

Password hint

Pin

Notes

Site Name

Site Address

Username

Password

Email

Password hint

Pin

Notes

Site Name
Site Address
Username
Password
Email
Password hint
Pin
Notes

Site Name
Site Address
Username
Password
Email
Password hint
Pin
Notes

Site Name
Site Address
Username
Password
Email
Password hint
Pin
Notes

O-P

Q-R

S-T

U-V

W-X

Y-Z

Site Name

Site Address

Username

Password

Email

Password hint

Pin

Notes

Site Name

Site Address

Username

Password

Email

Password hint

Pin

Notes

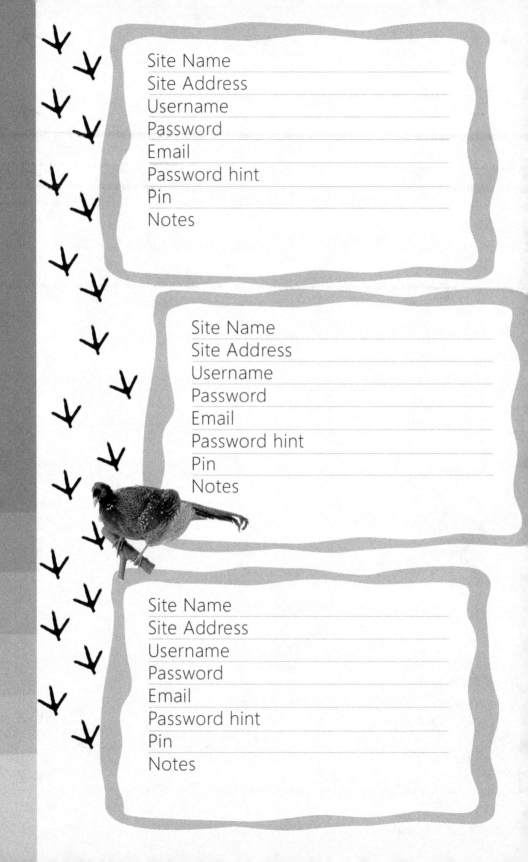

Site Name

Site Address

Username

Password

Email

Password hint

Pin

Notes

Site Name
Site Address
Username
Password
Email
Password hint
Pin
Notes

Site Name
Site Address
Username
Password
Email
Password hint
Pin
Notes

Site Name
Site Address
Username
Password
Email
Password hint
Pin
Notes

O-P

Q-R

S-T

U-V

W-X

Y-Z

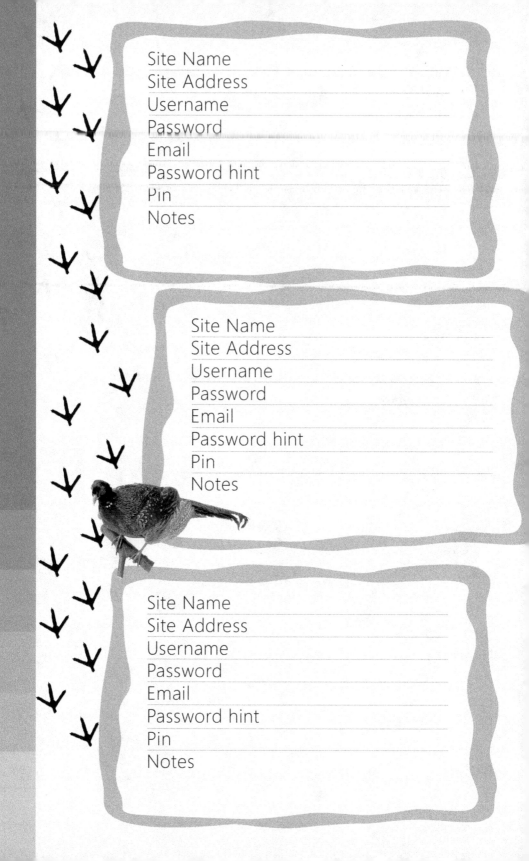

Site Name
Site Address
Username
Password
Email
Password hint
Pin
Notes

Site Name
Site Address
Username
Password
Email
Password hint
Pin
Notes

Site Name
Site Address
Username
Password
Email
Password hint
Pin
Notes

Site Name

Site Address

Username

Password

Email

Password hint

Pin

Notes

Site Name

Site Address

Username

Password

Email

Password hint

Pin

Notes

Site Name

Site Address

Username

Password

Email

Password hint

Pin

Notes

O-P

Q-R

S-T

U-V

W-X

Y-Z

Site Name

Site Address

Username

Password

Email

Password hint

Pin

Notes

Site Name

Site Address

Username

Password

Email

Password hint

Pin

Notes

Site Name

Site Address

Username

Password

Email

Password hint

Pin

Notes

Site Name

Site Address

Username

Password

Email

Password hint

Pin

Notes

Site Name

Site Address

Username

Password

Email

Password hint

Pin

Notes

Site Name

Site Address

Username

Password

Email

Password hint

Pin

Notes

O-P

Q-R

S-T

U-V

W-X

Y-Z

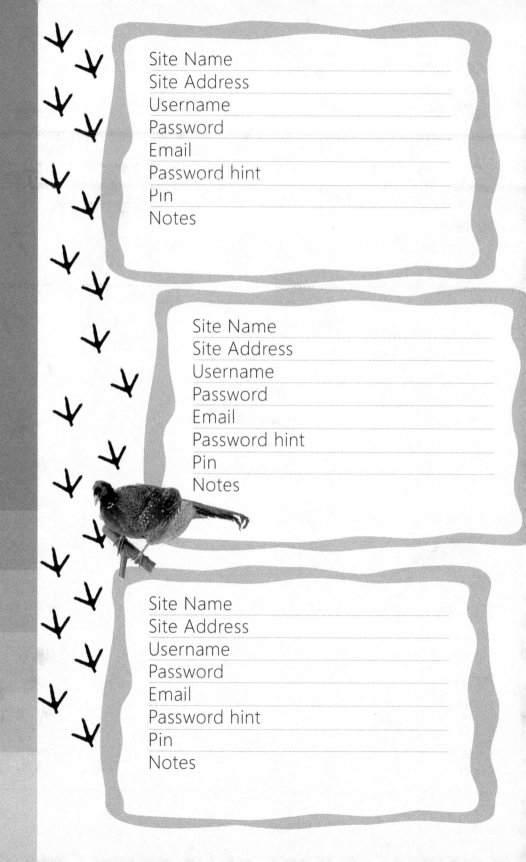

Site Name

Site Address

Username

Password

Email

Password hint

Pin

Notes

Site Name

Site Address

Username

Password

Email

Password hint

Pin

Notes

Site Name

Site Address

Username

Password

Email

Password hint

Pin

Notes

Site Name
Site Address
Username
Password
Email
Password hint
Pin
Notes

Site Name
Site Address
Username
Password
Email
Password hint
Pin
Notes

Site Name
Site Address
Username
Password
Email
Password hint
Pin
Notes

O-P

Q-R

S-T

U-V

W-X

Y-Z

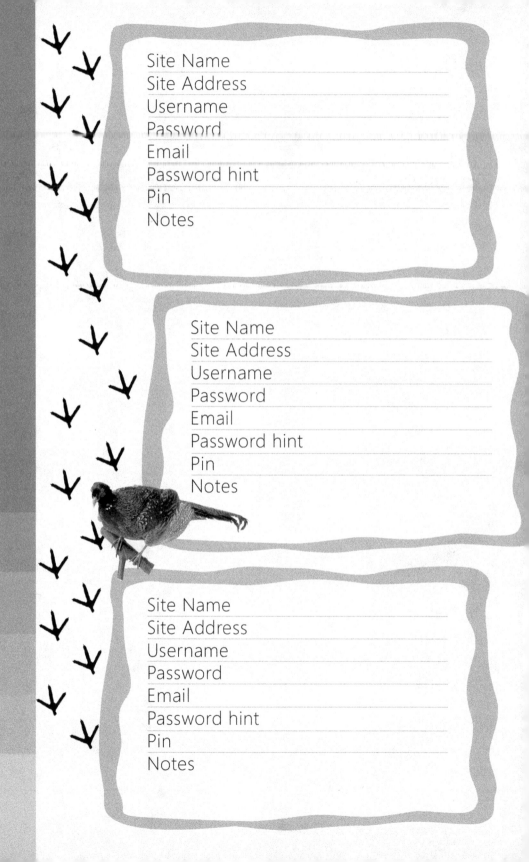

Site Name

Site Address

Username

Password

Email

Password hint

Pin

Notes

Site Name

Site Address

Username

Password

Email

Password hint

Pin

Notes

Site Name

Site Address

Username

Password

Email

Password hint

Pin

Notes

Download a printable copy

You can download and print this guide as a PDF by clicking on the link below and typing in the password.

There are fewer pages in the PDF than the paperback but you can print out extra pages for what you want when you need them so you don't waste ink on pages you don't require. It doesn't matter if you change a password or make a mistake, recycle the page and print out a new one!

The PDF size is US letter. This means that it can be printed and put in a ring binder. The printed password book will work best in clear plastic wallets in a ring binder so you can put the pages back to back and see the tabs clearly.

Visit:

http://cericlark.com/chirppdf

...and type in this password:
Chirpster

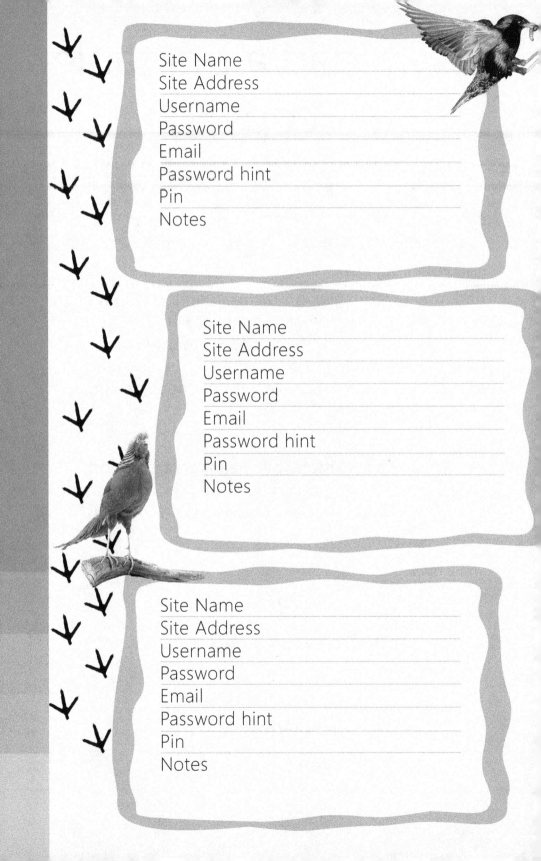

Site Name
Site Address
Username
Password
Email
Password hint
Pin
Notes

Site Name
Site Address
Username
Password
Email
Password hint
Pin
Notes

Site Name
Site Address
Username
Password
Email
Password hint
Pin
Notes

Site Name

Site Address

Username

Password

Email

Password hint

Pin

Notes

Site Name

Site Address

Username

Password

Email

Password hint

Pin

Notes

Site Name

Site Address

Username

Password

Email

Password hint

Pin

Notes

Q-R

S-T

U-V

W-X

Y-Z

Site Name

Site Address

Username

Password

Email

Password hint

Pin

Notes

Site Name

Site Address

Username

Password

Email

Password hint

Pin

Notes

Site Name

Site Address

Username

Password

Email

Password hint

Pin

Notes

Site Name

Site Address

Username

Password

Email

Password hint

Pin

Notes

Site Name

Site Address

Username

Password

Email

Password hint

Pin

Notes

Site Name

Site Address

Username

Password

Email

Password hint

Pin

Notes

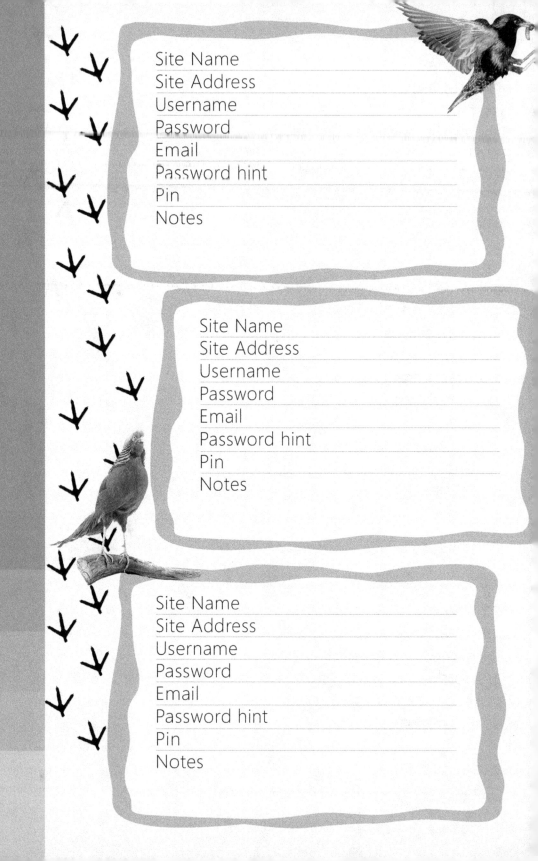

Site Name

Site Address

Username

Password

Email

Password hint

Pin

Notes

Site Name

Site Address

Username

Password

Email

Password hint

Pin

Notes

Site Name

Site Address

Username

Password

Email

Password hint

Pin

Notes

Site Name
Site Address
Username
Password
Email
Password hint
Pin
Notes

Site Name
Site Address
Username
Password
Email
Password hint
Pin
Notes

Site Name
Site Address
Username
Password
Email
Password hint
Pin
Notes

Q-R

S-T

U-V

W-X

Y-Z

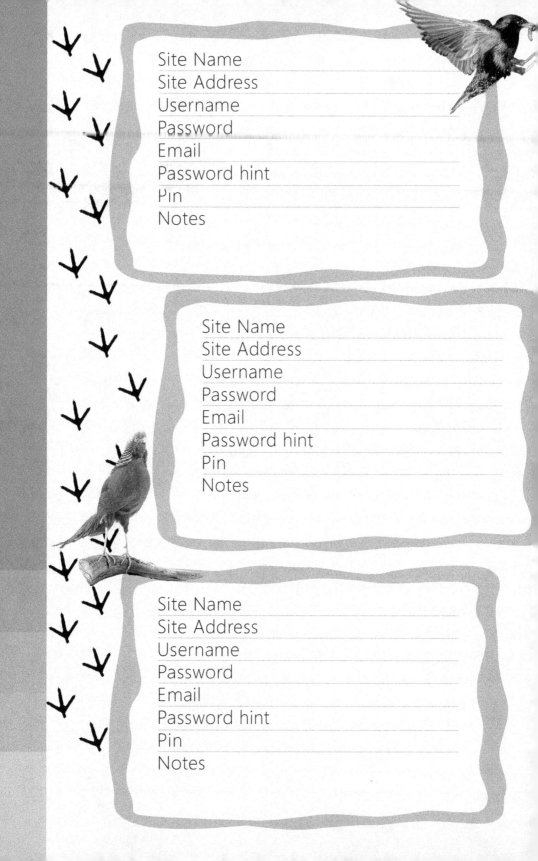

Site Name

Site Address

Username

Password

Email

Password hint

Pin

Notes

Site Name

Site Address

Username

Password

Email

Password hint

Pin

Notes

Site Name

Site Address

Username

Password

Email

Password hint

Pin

Notes

Site Name
Site Address
Username
Password
Email
Password hint
Pin
Notes

Site Name
Site Address
Username
Password
Email
Password hint
Pin
Notes

Site Name
Site Address
Username
Password
Email
Password hint
Pin
Notes

Q-R

S-T

U-V

W-X

Y-Z

Site Name

Site Address

Username

Password

Email

Password hint

Pin

Notes

Site Name

Site Address

Username

Password

Email

Password hint

Pin

Notes

Site Name

Site Address

Username

Password

Email

Password hint

Pin

Notes

Site Name
Site Address
Username
Password
Email
Password hint
Pin
Notes

Site Name
Site Address
Username
Password
Email
Password hint
Pin
Notes

Site Name
Site Address
Username
Password
Email
Password hint
Pin
Notes

Q-R

S-T

U-V

W-X

Y-Z

Site Name
Site Address
Username
Password
Email
Password hint
Pin
Notes

Site Name
Site Address
Username
Password
Email
Password hint
Pin
Notes

Site Name
Site Address
Username
Password
Email
Password hint
Pin
Notes

Site Name
Site Address
Username
Password
Email
Password hint
Pin
Notes

Site Name
Site Address
Username
Password
Email
Password hint
Pin
Notes

Site Name
Site Address
Username
Password
Email
Password hint
Pin
Notes

Site Name
Site Address
Username
Password
Email
Password hint
Pin
Notes

Site Name
Site Address
Username
Password
Email
Password hint
Pin
Notes

Site Name
Site Address
Username
Password
Email
Password hint
Pin
Notes

Site Name
Site Address
Username
Password
Email
Password hint
Pin
Notes

Site Name
Site Address
Username
Password
Email
Password hint
Pin
Notes

Site Name
Site Address
Username
Password
Email
Password hint
Pin
Notes

S-T

U-V

W-X

Y-Z

Site Name
Site Address
Username
Password
Email
Password hint
Pin
Notes

Site Name
Site Address
Username
Password
Email
Password hint
Pin
Notes

Site Name
Site Address
Username
Password
Email
Password hint
Pin
Notes

Site Name
Site Address
Username
Password
Email
Password hint
Pin
Notes

Site Name
Site Address
Username
Password
Email
Password hint
Pin
Notes

Site Name
Site Address
Username
Password
Email
Password hint
Pin
Notes

S-T

U-V

W-X

Y-Z

Site Name

Site Address

Username

Password

Email

Password hint

Pin

Notes

Site Name

Site Address

Username

Password

Email

Password hint

Pin

Notes

Site Name

Site Address

Username

Password

Email

Password hint

Pin

Notes

Site Name
Site Address
Username
Password
Email
Password hint
Pin
Notes

Site Name
Site Address
Username
Password
Email
Password hint
Pin
Notes

Site Name
Site Address
Username
Password
Email
Password hint
Pin
Notes

S-T

U-V

W-X

Y-Z

Site Name
Site Address
Username
Password
Email
Password hint
Pin
Notes

Site Name
Site Address
Username
Password
Email
Password hint
Pin
Notes

Site Name
Site Address
Username
Password
Email
Password hint
Pin
Notes

Site Name

Site Address

Username

Password

Email

Password hint

Pin

Notes

Site Name

Site Address

Username

Password

Email

Password hint

Pin

Notes

Site Name

Site Address

Username

Password

Email

Password hint

Pin

Notes

S-T

U-V

W-X

Y-Z

Site Name

Site Address

Username

Password

Email

Password hint

Pin

Notes

Site Name

Site Address

Username

Password

Email

Password hint

Pin

Notes

Site Name

Site Address

Username

Password

Email

Password hint

Pin

Notes

Site Name
Site Address
Username
Password
Email
Password hint
Pin
Notes

Site Name
Site Address
Username
Password
Email
Password hint
Pin
Notes

Site Name
Site Address
Username
Password
Email
Password hint
Pin
Notes

U-V

W-X

Y-Z

Site Name

Site Address

Username

Password

Email

Password hint

Pin

Notes

Site Name

Site Address

Username

Password

Email

Password hint

Pin

Notes

Site Name

Site Address

Username

Password

Email

Password hint

Pin

Notes

Site Name
Site Address
Username
Password
Email
Password hint
Pin
Notes

Site Name
Site Address
Username
Password
Email
Password hint
Pin
Notes

Site Name
Site Address
Username
Password
Email
Password hint
Pin
Notes

U-V

W-X

Y-Z

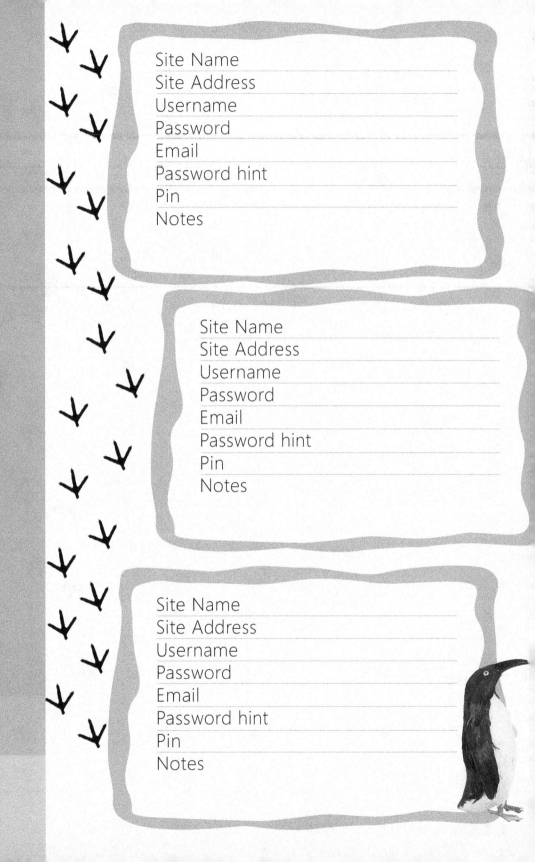

Site Name

Site Address

Username

Password

Email

Password hint

Pin

Notes

Site Name

Site Address

Username

Password

Email

Password hint

Pin

Notes

Site Name

Site Address

Username

Password

Email

Password hint

Pin

Notes

Site Name
Site Address
Username
Password
Email
Password hint
Pin
Notes

Site Name
Site Address
Username
Password
Email
Password hint
Pin
Notes

Site Name
Site Address
Username
Password
Email
Password hint
Pin
Notes

U-V

W-X

Y-Z

Site Name

Site Address

Username

Password

Email

Password hint

Pin

Notes

Site Name

Site Address

Username

Password

Email

Password hint

Pin

Notes

Site Name

Site Address

Username

Password

Email

Password hint

Pin

Notes

Site Name
Site Address
Username
Password
Email
Password hint
Pin
Notes

Site Name
Site Address
Username
Password
Email
Password hint
Pin
Notes

Site Name
Site Address
Username
Password
Email
Password hint
Pin
Notes

U-V

W-X

Y-Z

Site Name
Site Address
Username
Password
Email
Password hint
Pin
Notes

Site Name
Site Address
Username
Password
Email
Password hint
Pin
Notes

Site Name
Site Address
Username
Password
Email
Password hint
Pin
Notes

Site Name
Site Address
Username
Password
Email
Password hint
Pin
Notes

Site Name
Site Address
Username
Password
Email
Password hint
Pin
Notes

Site Name
Site Address
Username
Password
Email
Password hint
Pin
Notes

U-V

W-X

Y-Z

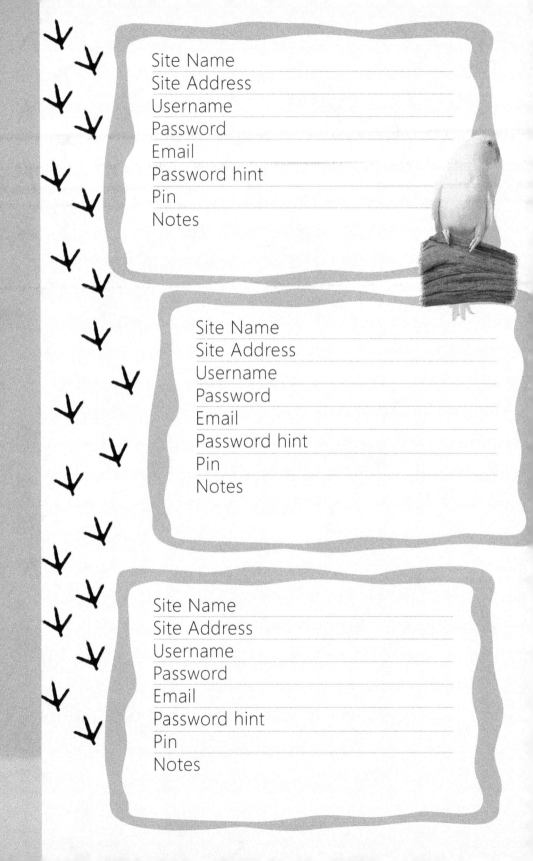

Site Name

Site Address

Username

Password

Email

Password hint

Pin

Notes

Site Name

Site Address

Username

Password

Email

Password hint

Pin

Notes

Site Name

Site Address

Username

Password

Email

Password hint

Pin

Notes

Site Name
Site Address
Username
Password
Email
Password hint
Pin
Notes

Site Name *Wells Frago*
Site Address
Username
Password *Butt 3287*
Email
Password hint
Pin
Notes *Bankaccount*

Site Name
Site Address
Username
Password
Email
Password hint
Pin
Notes

W-X

Y-Z

Site Name
Site Address
Username
Password
Email
Password hint
Pin
Notes

Site Name
Site Address
Username
Password
Email
Password hint
Pin
Notes

Site Name
Site Address
Username
Password
Email
Password hint
Pin
Notes

Site Name

Site Address

Username

Password

Email

Password hint

Pin

Notes

Site Name

Site Address

Username

Password

Email

Password hint

Pin

Notes

Site Name

Site Address

Username

Password

Email

Password hint

Pin

Notes

W-X

Y-Z

Site Name

Site Address

Username

Password

Email

Password hint

Pin

Notes

Site Name

Site Address

Username

Password

Email

Password hint

Pin

Notes

Site Name

Site Address

Username

Password

Email

Password hint

Pin

Notes

Site Name
Site Address
Username
Password
Email
Password hint
Pin
Notes

Site Name
Site Address
Username
Password
Email
Password hint
Pin
Notes

Site Name
Site Address
Username
Password
Email
Password hint
Pin
Notes

W-X

Y-Z

Site Name

Site Address

Username

Password

Email

Password hint

Pin

Notes

Site Name

Site Address

Username

Password

Email

Password hint

Pin

Notes

Site Name

Site Address

Username

Password

Email

Password hint

Pin

Notes

Site Name

Site Address

Username

Password

Email

Password hint

Pin

Notes

Site Name

Site Address

Username

Password

Email

Password hint

Pin

Notes

Site Name

Site Address

Username

Password

Email

Password hint

Pin

Notes

W-X

Y-Z

Site Name

Site Address

Username

Password

Email

Password hint

Pin

Notes

Site Name

Site Address

Username

Password

Email

Password hint

Pin

Notes

Site Name

Site Address

Username

Password

Email

Password hint

Pin

Notes

Site Name

Site Address

Username

Password

Email

Password hint

Pin

Notes

Site Name

Site Address

Username

Password

Email

Password hint

Pin

Notes

Site Name

Site Address

Username

Password

Email

Password hint

Pin

Notes

Site Name

Site Address

Username

Password

Email

Password hint

Pin

Notes

Site Name

Site Address

Username

Password

Email

Password hint

Pin

Notes

Site Name

Site Address

Username

Password

Email

Password hint

Pin

Notes

Site Name
Site Address
Username
Password
Email
Password hint
Pin
Notes

Site Name
Site Address
Username
Password
Email
Password hint
Pin
Notes

Site Name
Site Address
Username
Password
Email
Password hint
Pin
Notes

Y-Z

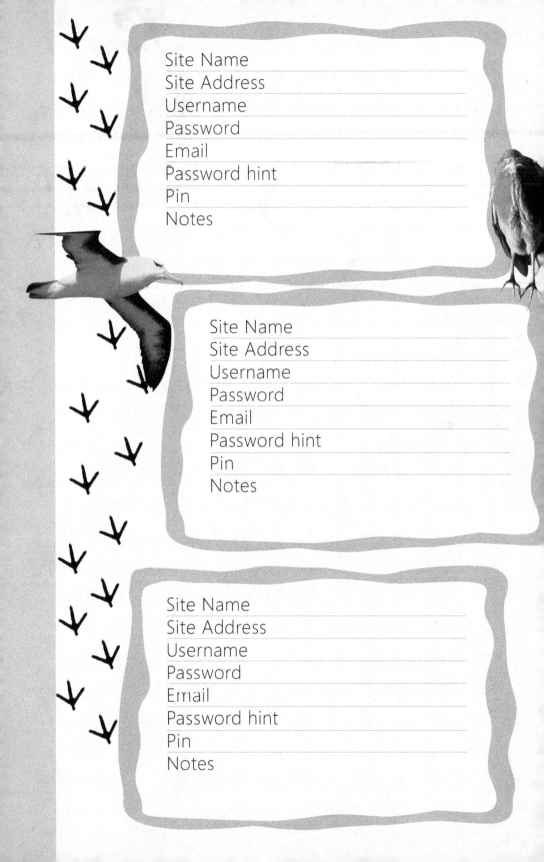

Site Name
Site Address
Username
Password
Email
Password hint
Pin
Notes

Site Name
Site Address
Username
Password
Email
Password hint
Pin
Notes

Site Name
Site Address
Username
Password
Email
Password hint
Pin
Notes

Site Name
Site Address
Username
Password
Email
Password hint
Pin
Notes

Site Name
Site Address
Username
Password
Email
Password hint
Pin
Notes

Site Name
Site Address
Username
Password
Email
Password hint
Pin
Notes

Y-Z

Site Name

Site Address

Username

Password

Email

Password hint

Pin

Notes

Site Name

Site Address

Username

Password

Email

Password hint

Pin

Notes

Site Name

Site Address

Username

Password

Email

Password hint

Pin

Notes

Site Name
Site Address
Username
Password
Email
Password hint
Pin
Notes

Site Name
Site Address
Username
Password
Email
Password hint
Pin
Notes

Site Name
Site Address
Username
Password
Email
Password hint
Pin
Notes

Y-Z

Site Name

Site Address

Username

Password

Email

Password hint

Pin

Notes

Site Name

Site Address

Username

Password

Email

Password hint

Pin

Notes

Site Name

Site Address

Username

Password

Email

Password hint

Pin

Notes

Site Name
Site Address
Username
Password
Email
Password hint
Pin
Notes

Site Name
Site Address
Username
Password
Email
Password hint
Pin
Notes

Site Name
Site Address
Username
Password
Email
Password hint
Pin
Notes

Y-Z

Site Name

Site Address

Username

Password

Email

Password hint

Pin

Notes

Site Name

Site Address

Username

Password

Email

Password hint

Pin

Notes

Site Name

Site Address

Username

Password

Email

Password hint

Pin

Notes

Site Name
Site Address
Username
Password
Email
Password hint
Pin
Notes

Site Name
Site Address
Username
Password
Email
Password hint
Pin
Notes

Site Name
Site Address
Username
Password
Email
Password hint
Pin
Notes

Y-Z

Internet Access Settings

Broadband Modem

Model

Serial number

Mac Address

Admin URL/IP Address

WAN IP Address

Username

Password

Notes

Router/ Wireless Access

*Useful if you need to reset your router or wireless access

Model

Serial Number

Default Username*

Default Password*

Your URL/IP Address

Your Username

Your Password

Notes

WAN Settings

Mac Address

Host Name

Domain Name

IP Address

Subnet Mask

Default Gateway

DNS

Notes

LAN Settings

IP Address

Subnet Mask

DHCP Range

Notes

Wireless Settings

SSID
(Wireless name)

Channel

Security Mode

WPA Shared Key

WEP Passphrase

Notes

Software Licenses

Software
License number
Purchased on
Notes

Software
License number
Purchased on
Notes

Software
License number
Purchased on
Notes

Software
License number
Purchased on
Notes

Software
License number
Purchased on
Notes

Software
License number
Purchased on
Notes

Software
License number
Purchased on
Notes

Software
License number
Purchased on
Notes

Software

License number

Purchased on

Notes

Software

License number

Purchased on

Notes

Software

License number

Purchased on

Notes

Software

License number

Purchased on

Notes

Software

License number

Purchased on

Notes

Software

License number

Purchased on

Notes

Software

License number

Purchased on

Notes

Software

License number

Purchased on

Notes

Notes

Notes

Notes

Bank ##

Rot # ⊙ 21 2000 25

Disguised Password Books

Are you always losing usernames and passwords? Would you like one convenient place to put all your login information?

Take a look at these attractive themed password books available now from Amazon.

BOOKS IN THE SERIES...

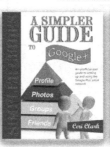

CPSIA information can be obtained
at www.ICGtesting.com
Printed in the USA
BVHW042147270520
580459BV00014B/393